CW01509997

Atlanta

in 3 Days:

The Definitive Tourist Guide Book That
Helps You Travel Smart and Save Time

Finest City Guides

Book Description

"Atlanta in 3 Days" will take you to all the best that this bright and energetic city provides. If you only have a few days or so to spend here, you'll enjoy the popular attractions and festivals we profile here.

We also provide practical and important information about getting around on public transit, tipping, and where to stay and eat, whatever your budget.

Atlanta offers you new things to discover every day. From tourist attractions like the Georgia Aquarium to areas that aren't as well known, you'll find all the attractions in this guide are worthwhile to someone in your family or group.

The People of Atlanta, Georgia

Technically, the population of Atlanta is only about 420,000. But when you add in the metropolitan area, the total soars to over five million!

Atlanta is over 50% African American or Black, 35% White, 5% Hispanic, 3% Asian and less than .25% Native American. The cost of living in Atlanta is 6% lower than in most large American metro areas.

Atlanta boasts one of the highest populations in LGBT per capita, placing it third among the major cities in the United States. Over 12% of the total population of Atlanta identifies itself as bisexual, gay or lesbian. Just over 7% of people who live in Atlanta were born overseas.

Atlanta is one of the United States' largest cities to have an African American majority. It has been known for many years as a center for African American culture, power and education.

Language

From Atlanta's total population that are five years of age and older, 83% speak English only in the home. 9% speak Spanish and 4% speak other Indo-European languages.

The dialect of Atlanta is a variation of the language known as Southern American English. Because many companies have their corporate headquarters in or near Atlanta, the city has attracted in-country migrants from other US areas. In 2003, Atlanta Magazine itself concluded that the city was de-Southernized.

Culinary Delights

Atlanta is just a little defensive about the varieties of its food. But it doesn't need to be. In the last 10 years, Atlanta has happily experienced an upgrade in culinary ambition. Their menus reflect a new sophisticated Southern menu, which is centered on the farm but most often experienced within the city.

The restaurants in Atlanta today are founded on Atlanta chefs including Anne Quatrano and Scott

Peacock. It is the home city for eight contenders in the much-coveted "Top Chef" franchise, and it recently hosted a huge wine and food festival for products of the South, which was sponsored by Travel & Leisure and Food & Wine magazines.

Southern food in Atlanta today is driven by farm grown foods. The chefs are exploring ways to mix trend and technique with its roots in the country. The central role is played by vegetables.

More than just great food, Atlanta expresses a unique intimacy at your table that feels like Italy in its love and generosity. Atlanta is a place where people love to eat the local recipes and things are worked on at the restaurant table.

Holidays

Atlanta celebrates all of the traditional holidays in the United States. They have parades on Saint Patrick's Day and fireworks on the 4th of July. The Peach drop is their end of the year party.

Religious Beliefs

Atlanta religion has been centered historically on Protestant Christianity, but it involves many faiths now, due to the increasingly international population. The Catholic Church has grown in recent years.

Metro Atlanta has numerous national and ethnic Christian congregations, including Indian and Korean churches. The larger of non-Christian faiths in Atlanta include Hinduism, Judaism and Islam. There are more than 1,000 houses of worship in Atlanta.

Here is a quick preview of what you will learn in this tourist guide:

- Helpful information about Atlanta
- Flying into the city
- Transportation tips in town
- Why Atlanta is such a vibrant tourist spot and what you will find most remarkable about it
- Information on luxury and budget accommodations and what you'll get for your money
- The currency used in Atlanta
- Tourist attractions you should make time to see
- Other attractions for entertainment and culture
- Events that may be running during your stay
- Tips on the best places to eat & drink for all price points, whether you want simple fare, worldwide dishes or Southern flavor

Table of Contents

1. Introduction

As the largest city and the capital of Georgia, USA, Atlanta is a major cultural and financial force in the South. The metro area covers over 6,000 square miles, including over 100 municipalities.

People from all over the US, in addition to immigrants from other countries, flock to the job opportunities, mild climate and physical beauty. In Atlanta, you'll find the graciousness of the old South, and also an ambition for dominance and expansion. The city has a vital position in national commerce, and international commerce, as well.

A Brief History of Atlanta

The first settler in Atlanta built a cabin in 1833 on land that had belonged to the Creek tribe. Atlanta's first name was Terminus, when founded in 1837, since it made up one end of the Western and Atlantic railroad line. The town was incorporated in 1843 as Marthasville and was not named Atlanta until 1845.

Atlanta was a marketing and rail hub, and during the Civil War, was a supply and communication center. The city fell to General Sherman in 1864. Most of the city was burned in November, before Sherman's march to the sea.

Atlanta was rebuilt rapidly, and thrived as both an industrial and commercial center. It became Georgia's capital in 1877. Expositions and conventions drew attention to the strategic position and growth of the city.

The actual city of Atlanta has steadily lost residents to the expanding suburbs in the 20th and 21st centuries. The urban areas contain more than 10 times as many people as the relatively small city proper.

What does Atlanta Offer its Visitors?

Regardless of what you're interested in, Atlanta has something for you. From rock climbing and other sports to fine dining, great shopping and a bustling night life, Atlanta can keep you busy for as long as you can stay. Its diversity and its people are highlights of any trip to the area.

2. Key Information about Atlanta

Money Matters

Atlanta uses the US dollar, symbolized as $ or USD or US$. The paper money consists of dollar bills described as Federal Reserve Notes.

Coins in US currency include the quarter (25 cents or ¼ of $1), dime (10 cents), nickel (5 cents) and penny (one cent).

The U.S. dollar is the most used currency in transactions around the world, and the primary reserve currency for the world. Some other countries even use the U.S. Dollar as their own official currency.

Tipping

There are many US customs that travelers find confusing, but none are more so than tipping. Residents of the US treat gratuities as a normal fact of like, just like states that have sales tax. To foreign visitors, tipping can cause some anxiety.

If you are not accustomed to tipping, perhaps it would help you to know that the federal minimum wage for US adults is only $7.25 per hour. In businesses like restaurants, where tipping is the norm, employers can pay their workers as low as $2.13 per hour! So, if they don't get tips, they can't pay the bills. Refusing to tip doesn't hurt the restaurants, but only the low-paid waitresses and waiters.

Restaurant Tipping

No one can force you to pay your waiter a tip when you dine, but it is sometimes added into the bill on larger groups. Count on it being added in if your party has six or more people.

If the tips are already added when you pay your bill, you don't need to do anything else. If no tip is in the bill, you can leave some money on the table.

If you eat at a fast food restaurant, no tips are left. If it is a modest diner or an upmarket eatery, the tip is 15-20% for good service. If you are in big cities like New York or Los Angeles it's closer to 20-30%. It is not acceptable to withhold your tip unless the service or food was poor. If the service or food was reallllly bad, leave a couple pennies as your tip. That's symbolic and it will be understood.

When you dine in a fancy, exclusive restaurant, your tip will be 25% of your bill handed to the waiter. He will divide it among his support staff. You can also tip the maitre'd for a great table, or the sommelier if they suggest a good wine. Bartenders are tipped for every drink they serve.

In coffee shops, and they are everywhere, you may see tip jars, but most people pay with credit or debit cards. People don't generally leave tips unless the service was very fast.

Hotel Tipping

If someone opens the door for you at your hotel, no tip is needed. If he carries your bags, his tip should be about $2 to $3 per bag.

If your hotel has a concierge, you don't have to tip just for friendly service. However, if they serve you in an individual way, like hiring a car or booking a side trip, you should acknowledge this with a tip of $10-$20, paid when you leave.

One instance where tips impact service quality is in housekeeping. Leave $2-$5 on the pillow each morning, with a note of thanks. This means that cleaners will be more diligent for the remainder of your stay.

3. Transport to and in Atlanta

Getting to Atlanta by Plane

Known in the city as just "Atlanta Airport", the actual name of the airport is the Hartsfield–Jackson Atlanta International Airport. It's located seven miles south of Atlanta's central business district.

This is the busiest airport in the world nearly every year since 1998, based on passenger traffic. It routinely accommodates over 260,000 passengers a day. While it is home to major US airlines, Atlanta is also a major international hub.

Getting to Atlanta (the city) from the Airport

There are numerous motels, hotels and inns close to Hartsfield-Jackson Atlanta International Airport (ATL). Here are the hotels and inns that are happy to provide a free shuttle service going to or from ATL airport.

Service by MARTA

Hartsfield–Jackson has its own station on the city's rapid transit train system, MARTA. It's located on the west end of the main building.

Atlanta Cabs

Unlike New York City or other large cities, who have one approved taxi company, choosing a cab company in Atlanta can take you through a whole page on Yelp.com. In fact, there are 22 taxi companies in the Atlanta metro area!

Here are the main companies offering service in the Atlanta metro area. Most accept credit cards, in addition to cash. Atlanta has Uber vehicles, as well.

- Atlanta Checker Cab Co Inc.
  (404) 351-1111
- A & B Airport cab
  (866) 206-2562
- Style Taxi & Limousine
  (770) 522-8294
- Gold Cab & Airport Transportation
  (404) 941-8423
- Tele Taxi
  (770) 449-9499

Payment and Tipping for Taxi's

If you've never visited Atlanta, you may wonder how much it'll cost to get from one point to another by taxi. It's not difficult to calculate.

1. When you are traveling within a single zone (like midtown, downtown or Buckhead) the flat fee is $8.00 for the first person and $2.00 for each additional person.

2. When you are traveling from the airport to a specific zone (midtown, downtown or Buckhead) you will pay a flat fee:

From ATL to Downtown $30.00
From ATL to Midtown $32.00
From ATL to Buckhead $38.00

3. In any other case, the rate is:

$2.50 for the 1st 1/8th mile or less
$0.25 for each additional 1/8th of a mile
$21.00 for each hour waiting time ($0.35/min)

Tipping in taxis is more confusing than that in restaurants. You'll sometimes find a seat-back display that shows you "default tipping" at the end of your trip, and it may run up to 25-30%.

Not many people actually pay 30% in a taxi. It's more subjective and should be more than 15% if your driver did an excellent job in getting you swiftly and safely to your end point.

Taxi Precautions

Before getting into a taxi, make sure that they have a typical TAXI sign, and that the photo on the registration matches your potential driver.

Atlanta Rental Cars

Unlike many tourist cities, you can benefit by renting a car when you arrive in Atlanta. There are major dealers at the airport, including Hertz, Enterprise and Dollar. The city sprawls over a large area, so having a rental car can be cheaper than taking taxi cabs. Be aware though, if you are staying downtown, it may be difficult to find parking spots available.

Public Transport in Atlanta

Local Atlanta Public Transit (MARTA)

The Metropolitan Atlanta Rapid Transit Authority (MARTA) operates the public transportation system in Atlanta. It offers buses and trains.

MARTA is a rider-friendly system, whether you're visiting, commuting, biking, disabled or bilingual. They don't have tokens or passes anymore. Just tap your Breeze Card on the blue target at the station where you're boarding.

Using the MARTA system

- **Get a Breeze Card**

As a rider, you need a Breeze Card if you want to use a train or bus. Purchase fare for your card at any rail station (by machine) or at a MARTA Ridestore.

- **Load your Breeze Card**

You can load your card from the MARTA website, at MARTA Ridestores and at any Breeze vending machine.

- **Exiting to Transfer or at your Destination**

Tap your Breeze Card on the blue target to exit a train station. You can transfer at no cost by tapping the card again immediately on the bus or train at the station where you exit.

4. Accommodations

Luxury Hotels

There is no shortage of luxury hotels in Atlanta. The city is geared for tourism, and the information below should help you make your search for that perfect hotel a bit easier. Prices for luxury hotels in Atlanta generally run from $505 to $2000+ per night.

St. Regis Hotel Atlanta – $935 and up

Experience the original art and custom furnishings of one of Atlanta's finest hotels. You'll have a deck with a view to die for. Each detail is enhanced by the St. Regis touch.

Enjoy the Remede Spa to rejuvenate, or linger at the Pool Piazza. Relax in a Jacuzzi. Snuggle by the outdoor fireplace with cascading waterfall, or unwind and lose your worries at the poolside bar.

Four Seasons Hotel Atlanta - $499 - $2,000 per night

The Four Seasons has dedicated itself to making your travel experience perfect. They offer exceptional innovation and high hospitality standards. The surroundings are elegant and the caring, personalized staff are there 24 hours, to meet your every need.

Four Seasons offers elegance for people who appreciate the best. The culture of Four Seasons is perfectly personified by their employees – they share the focus to offer only the best service. The company leads the hospitality industry with innovations that make leisure travel more comfortable and business travel hassle-free.

Mandarin Oriental Hotel Atlanta- $505 USD and up

The Mandarin Oriental is located in Buckhead, one of the most elite areas of Atlanta. It combines elegant luxury with easy access to all of Atlanta. It is within easy walking distance to not one, but three world-class destinations for shopping.

This is the perfect place for you to stay, whether you're enjoying a romantic vacation or relaxing for a bit during a business trip. You'll have easy access to the top attractions in Atlanta, including the High Museum of Art, the Atlanta Botanical Garden and Piedmont Park.

After a night or day in town, unwind in the spa, with 15,000 square feet in which to relax. Lie down and loosen up with a personalized massage, or enjoy the indoor lap pool, steam room, fitness center and vitality pool.

Mid-Range Hotels in Atlanta

If you'd rather save some money to spend on shopping or attractions than spend it on your lodging, you can find great rooms at mid-range Atlanta hotels. Some of them are still 5-stars! The rooms run from $239-$500 per night

The Grand Hyatt Atlanta Hotel in Buckhead - $239 USD and up

The Grand Hyatt in Buckhead is well-settled in this upscale Atlanta neighborhood. Southern hospitality will greet you at every turn. Spacious guestrooms include Hyatt Grand Beds™ and flat screen HDTV's. Enjoy the Japanese Zen Garden and then relish the renowned Southern style cuisine at Cassis.

W Hotel Atlanta Midtown – from $226 per night

With divine design and superb service, the W combines modern art influence with vintage architecture. The hotel is the location for the upscale club Whiskey Park and the Spice Market restaurant. When the day is done, unwind at the Bliss Spa, with 4,000 square feet of... well, the name says it all...Bliss.

Loews Atlanta Hotel – from $ 279 per night

Walk into the new and stylish atmosphere of The Loews Atlanta, where classic luxury meets contemporary Southern style. Leave your cares behind and book a soothing spa session. Enjoy the outstanding service and dine on delectable Southern dishes.

The suites at The Loews are designed to be spacious and well-designed for both relaxation and work on the go. The views from the floor to ceiling windows will inspire you.

Atlanta Hotels for the Budget-Conscious

If you're a busy tourist and spend minimal time in your hotel, why spend a big chunk of your budget on luxury accommodations? Budget-friendly Atlanta hotels give you some of the perks of mid-range hotels, at lower prices. Prices run from $50 to $150 & up per night.

Hawthorn Suites by Wyndham Atlanta Perimeter Center – from $150 per night

The Hawthorn Suites offer you lots for your money. They have a free hot and cold breakfast, with full fitness facilities and an outdoor pool for cooling off after a long day.If you're on the road for work, you'll appreciate the business center, conference space, and computer stations.

Hawthorn Suites has a front desk that's open 24 hours, full dry cleaning service and even a picnic area.

Ramada Marietta/Atlanta North – from $80 per night

Ramada Inn is known for offering weary travelers a place they can crash, whether they're traveling for fun or business. They have a free daily continental breakfast and a common area with free tea and coffee.

The indoor pool allows you to enjoy a bit of splashy fun regardless of the season. You'll also enjoy the fitness facilities, with spa tubs. If you're on a working holiday or a business trip, the Ramada offers conference space, a business center and a front desk that is staffed 24 hours a day.

Garden Plaza Hotel Atlanta Norcross – from $59 per night

The Garden Plaza has everything you'll need when you wind down after a long day of work or play. They have a free daily continental breakfast, and lots of extras. They include indoor and outdoor pools, golf lessons and fitness facilities. If you're into staying in shape, they also offer discounts at a full fitness center close by.

Airbnb's

There are well over 300 Airbnb's in the Atlanta Metropolitan area. From a quaint small apartment to an adult-sized treehouse, there is a type of accommodation that will suit anyone. Prices range from $49 to $360 and up.

5. Sightseeing

This helpful section gives you the highlights of a trip to Atlanta. These are places that, while "touristy", are still on everyone's "must see" list. There are tons of things to do while you're in town, but these are a few of the most popular activities.

The Georgia Aquarium

The Georgia Aquarium is among the most captivating and largest aquariums in the world. It has huge aquatic habitats and an abundant collection of aquatic life. It's not far to drive, either – it's right downtown.

You'll enjoy the displays, with over 10 million gallons of water. Watch the beluga whales and whale sharks, and enjoy the 4D aquatic theater. The Pier 225 Sea Lion Gallery and AT&T Dolphin Tales will entertain adults and children alike.

Martin Luther King Jr. National Historic Site

The National Park Service runs this historic site that many have found inspiring and memorable.

Martin Luther King Jr. was a giant, and this site showcases his amazing life. The exhibits offer realistic, unique glimpses into the years when Reverend King was living.

The décor, history and artifacts are fabulous. The house is authentic for the area and has the same furnishings it has when MLK Junior lived in it. The home is rich in culture and includes many important historical stories. The tour guides will share interesting facts that most people don't know.

Atlanta History Center

The History Center of Atlanta is found in the center of Buckhead, and invites you to explore the past of the city through exhibitions that have won nationwide acclaim.

The center is housed in two historic homes from the 1800's and 1900's and includes the Goizeta Gardens and the Museum of the Centennial Olympic Games. You can even tour the house known as the birth place of Gone with the Wind!

6. Eat & Drink

Countless Southern food type restaurants in Atlanta serve lots more than just fried green tomatoes, fried chicken and grits. The best restaurants feature new Southern cuisine, too. It rivals many family recipes.

Whether you dine at high-end restaurants or small and cozy destinations, discover your favorite foods of the South while you're in Atlanta.

The Atlanta restaurants in our guide are classified into three price points:

Expensive Prices (over $50 per person)
Moderate Prices ($31 to $50)
Inexpensive Prices (under $25)

Chops – Expensive

Chops is nothing less than an icon in Atlanta, well-known for its outstanding service and food. It is ranked in the Top 10 US Steakhouses. Their USDA prime aged beef and flown-in-fresh-every-day seafood are served in the warm comfort of their wood dining room.

At lower level, the Lobster Bar is a paradise for seafood lovers. Enjoy specialties like their famous Batter Fried Lobster Tail and the Savannah Lump Crab Cocktail. Savor a cocktail, or wine from their extensive list. Whether you are dining on vacation or with co-workers, eating at Chops will make a memorable impression. Note that proper dress is required.

Fogo de Chao Brazilian Steakhouse – Expensive

Fogo de Chão (fo-go dèe shoun) is a Brazilian steakhouse with authentic foods. Fogo began sharing their way to prepare meat in 1979 in Brazil. Today, their gaucho chefs are still expertly grilling each of 20 different cuts. They also offer continuous service, tableside.

You're invited to enjoy their gaucho chefs' delicious preparations, as well as their gourmet market table. They have an award-winning wine list and authentic side dishes inspired in Brazil.

Blue Ridge Grill – Expensive

Blue Ridge Grill Atlanta is a great American Grill in the setting of a mountain lodge. They specialize in hickory grilled prime steaks and fresh seafood. They also have a focus on using local ingredients.

Moderately Priced Restaurants

Canoe – Moderate

You'll find Canoe in the Vinings area of Atlanta, beside the Chattahoochee River near Buckhead. The gorgeous setting, riverside, makes it a great spot for meals, as well as receptions and parties.

Some of the most popular dishes at Canoe include Boneless T-bone Pork, Roasted Australian Lamb Chop and Peppercorn Crusted Block Island Swordfish.

Sun Dial Restaurant– Moderate

The Sun Dial is well known, since it rotates at 723 feet above Atlanta on Peachtree Street. As the city's only three-level dining complex, they offer panoramic 360 degree views of the city skyline. The food is seasonal contemporary American, using local ingredients.

The live jazz, splendid views and tantalizing food choices create an ambiance like no other restaurant in Atlanta. It's truly the ultimate dining experience in town.

Gypsy Kitchen – Moderate

This restaurant has drawn inspiration from Spain's culinary riches, infused with Indian and Moroccan influences. With interplay through the centuries between these foods, they inspire the Iberian fusion plates at Gypsy Kitchen.

Their beverages are as unique as their cuisine. Gypsy hand-crafted cocktails are alive with fresh juices and unique ingredients. The wine list will transport you to Spain and other Old World wine countries. Looking for beer? They have European beers and American craft beers to round out the choices.

Inexpensive Atlanta Restaurants

TRACE – Inexpensive

TRACE is located in the Midtown W Atlanta Hotel. It's a farm-to-table restaurant with Southern dining that features modern and classic twists on New South favorite dishes. Using local farms for ingredients in their Southern dishes, this is a restaurant that connects with the community by providing fresh, sourceable fare.

Kozmo Gastro Pub – Inexpensive

Kozmo is an urban-style, chic tavern that serves comfort cuisine, along with their rendition of the now-classic Kozmopolitan cocktail.

Among the food favorites at Kozmo, you'll find such varieties as Cheese Fondue, Tempura Shrimp & Sea Scallops and Braised Beef Empanadas.

Food 101 – Inexpensive

Food 101 serves hearty foods with urban polish and rural roots. Your dining experience will remind you of days long past. The menu offers classics with inventive twists. The eatery exudes comfort through foods and a relaxing atmosphere.

Among the favorites served at Food 101, you'll find Three Meat Meatloaf and Shrimp & Grits with onion, sausage and tomato gravy.

7. Culture and Entertainment

While Atlanta is located in the South, its culture is not strictly Southern any longer. This happened due to migrants from other areas in the United States, as well as more recent immigrants to the US, who made the Atlanta metro area their home. This has established Atlanta as a multi-cultural area.

Although Southern culture and tradition is a part of the cultural fabric of Atlanta, it is now the backdrop to one of America's most cosmopolitan areas. You will find these unique cultural combinations in the multi-ethnic domain along Buford Highway, the arts districts in Midtown and the quirky eastside neighborhoods of Atlanta.

High Museum of Art

The High Museum of Art is the premier museum for local and international traveling exhibits. The museum is a partner with the Louvre and MOMA, sharing the finest exhibits of modern painters and Old Masters.

The High Museum has car, clothing and jewelry shows. They house permanent Folk art collections and Southern outsider artists, along with African art.

The Tullie Smith House – Smith Family Farm

The Smith Family Farm features the Tullie Smith House. It was built originally in the 1840's, and is a plain plantation style home. It was built east of the city, and survived the destruction in the area during the US Civil War.

The Tullie Smith House was moved to the Atlanta History Center in the 1970's and is circled by a separate kitchen, barn, slave cabin, corncrib, smokehouse, blacksmith shop and dairy, along with slave gardens, flower, field, herb and vegetable gardens.

Cobb Energy Performing Arts Centre

The Cobb Energy Performing Arts Centre is the premier venue for performance in Atlanta. It houses Broadway shows, concerts, opera, ballet, comedy and educational shows, wedding receptions and other events.

The mission of this center is the creation of entertainment, cultural and educational experiences to promote more accessibility to the arts. They seek to foster partnerships in the community to unify the support of the arts in the region. The center was also designed to stimulate economic growth in the community, and inspire local individuals to increase their knowledge of the arts.

Entertainment Venues

World of Coca Cola

How interesting will it be to learn the story of Coke? Your kids, if they are along, will want to head right for the sample room, but hold them back for a bit, so you can do some learning, too.

The museum explains how Coca Cola began, and how the company functions today, all around the world. There are many interactive exhibits and of course, the tasting room. You've likely never even heard of all these different flavors from Coke, and you'll enjoy trying some for yourself.

CNN Center – Studio Tour

This is a popular tour for people traveling to Atlanta. It begins with the longest escalator in the world! You'll see how the news studio works, learn how to use the green screen, and go behind the scenes in the live studio and control room. You can even talk to the news anchor when they break for commercials!

Ponce City Market

This market is ever expanding, and if you visit more than once, a year or two apart, you'll find new shops and restaurants. Foodies love this market! Anything you can think of that's edible is probably found here. And if you like watching people, you could spend the whole day just doing that.

You'll find many diverse dinner options in the Food Hall. Whether you like seafood or steaks, you'll love the choices. Try a seltzer. Stay late and head for Skyline Park. You can see amazing Atlanta skyline views from there.

Atlanta Night-life

Atlanta natives love the night, and so will you! They have unique and fun attractions, renowned restaurants and tons of clubs where you can dance the night away.

Each area has its own eccentricities. Buckhead has a chic style, Little Five Points has its alternative scene, Virginia-Highland has a casual atmosphere and Midtown has a trendy vibe. The nightlife of Atlanta can fit anyone's style of letting loose.

The most popular area for nightlife is still Buckhead. This is true for locals and visitors alike. Buckhead clientele is largely upscale, so dress to impress.

Johnny's Hideaway Buckhorn

Johnny's Hideaway offers the best DJ's in Atlanta who spin hits from the 1950's all the way to today's music. It's all for your dancing and listening pleasure. Ladies' Night Wednesdays and All-request Mondays are their highlights. The restaurant serves food until the wee hours and they're open seven nights a week.

Cosmolava Night Club Midtown

Booked as the ultimate experience in Midtown, Cosmolava doesn't fail to deliver. They boast three levels and six bars, along with hot DJ's and VIP accommodations. Sip delicious cocktails while you mingle on the deck, which is visually nestled in the skyline of Midtown. Hit one of their four dance floors to the variety of music being spun –it includes Funk, 80's, Top 40 and mainstream music.

SkyLounge Downtown Atlanta

If you're in a sophisticated mood, check out the Skylounge, a rooftop lounge built atop the historic Glenn Hotel. It's right in the middle of downtown Atlanta's entertainment and business locale.

Sit back and relax. Enjoy the panoramic views of Atlanta while you sip hand-crafted fusion cocktails. It was even voted as one of the Top 23 Best Rooftop Lounges Worldwide by ABC.com.

8. Special Events in Atlanta

New Year's Day Climb
January 1 - 10:00 AM

Who needs a parade on New Year's Day? Spend the day working off the calories you drank the night before in the Stone Mountain Climb. The clean air is just what you need to clear your head.

MLK Day Commemoration
January 16, 2017

Arrive early at the Ebenezer Baptist Church for the Martin Luther King, Jr. Commemorative Service. It features keynote speakers and gospel artists.

Callanwolde Arts Festival
January 20-22, 2017

The Callanwolde Arts Festival is an indoor party held in a historic property in Atlanta. This festival is put on by artists for artists. This lets local artists have a voice in the operation of the festival.

The event features 80+ painters, jewelers, glass artists, metalwork artists, sculptors and photographers. They offer live demonstrations, gourmet food trucks, live acoustic music and dance and music performances.

Atlanta Mardi Gras Ball
February 18, 2017

The Atlanta Mardi Gras Ball is quite a festive party, to be sure. It pays homage to the tradition of Mardi Gras, and to New Orleans and Hurricane Katrina survivors. This event is in midtown at Le Fais Do~Do.

St. Patrick's Day Parade
March 11, 2017 (12:30 to 1:30 p.m.)

Here's the parade that locals wait for all year round. It features 2,000 Irish enthusiasts: musicians, dancers and viewers. You'll also see floats, marching bands and giant balloons on the parade route in Midtown.

Easter

Easter egg hunt in the garden
April 15, 2017

Bring your own basket – to fill with candy-filled Easter eggs. Have your kids meet the Easter Bunny! Enjoy the kids' activities and check out the baked goods at Callanwolde Fine Arts Center.

Art at the River - Easter
April 15, 2017

This Easter art fair on the Chattahoochee River offers a market of fine art, along with entertainment, a crafts corner and a food court. The fair is located at Simpsonwood Park in Peachtree Corners.

Memorial Day ceremonies
May, 2017

The Smyrna 2017 Memorial Day Ceremony starts at 9:30 a.m. at the 20th Century Veterans Memorial. It is a free ceremony.

The Roswell Remembers ceremony includes music, displays and food tents. You'll find it at City Hall. There is no charge for admission.

Fourth of July Fireworks Displays
July 4, 2017

Turner Field & Centennial Olympic Park will illuminate the sky over Atlanta with fireworks on the Fourth. You can enjoy fun and food from 6 pm until after the fireworks are over at Centennial Olympic Park, or choose to celebrate by rooting on the Atlanta Braves as they play at Turner Field.

Labor Day at the Mountain
September 3 - 5, 2016

Labor Day Weekend celebrates, as it was intended, everyday working heroes. Enjoy fireworks and a laser show from Stone Mountain Park.

Halloween

Atlanta loves Halloween. There are always all kinds of activities going on. From face painting to festivals and haunted houses, you'll find something for each person in your family.

One of the most famous haunted houses in the US, Netherworld, is in Atlanta. They also hold the Little Five Points Halloween Festival &

Parade. Six Flags over Georgia hosts Halloween spills, thrills, turns and tumbles. You can find almost anything ghoulish you might want to do in Atlanta.

Little 5 Points Halloween Festival & Parade

This is among the largest Halloween events in the US. Over 30,000 people pack the art, music and entertainment district each year for a parade as chilling and eclectic as any other you'll probably ever see.

Thanksgiving Race
November 23, 2017

Before you sit for your family feast, run off some calories in the Thanksgiving Day 5K or Half-Marathon. They are held near Turner Field.

Holiday Lights Thanksgiving

Thanksgiving night is a popular night for seeing Atlanta's holiday lights. One of the favorites is the Atlanta Botanical Gardens Garden Nights, Holiday Lights. Call in advance for tickets. You can see a free light display at Centennial Park.

The Christmas Season in Atlanta

Atlanta sparkles each holiday season, with delightful events. They feature Kwanzaa traditions, Hanukkah celebrations and Atlanta Christmas events.

Christmas Events that Light up the Night

Garden Lights, Holiday Nights is held at the Atlanta Botanical Garden and features over one million colorful lights. There is also a Festival of the SEAson at Georgia Aquarium and a Lighting of Atlantic Station, along with many others.

New Year's Eve

The Peach Drop in Atlanta is the largest Southeast New Year's celebration. The festivities begin at 7 pm with live music and thousands of New Year revelers. As the evening passes, the main stage lights up with life performances. The 800-pound Peach begins its descent right before midnight. After the Peach drops, enjoy the fireworks and confetti.

Festivals

SweetWater 420 Fest
April 2017 – Dates unannounced

SweetWater 420 fest is so much more than great music and great beer. The goal is to make positive changes in our lives and the ways in which we affect the planet.

SweetWater Brewing Co. in Atlanta presents this festival. It is among the most popular annual events in the area. The lineup includes local artists, musicians and comedians.

During the festival, there is also a corn hole tournament, a 5K race and lots of ice-cold beer. Proceeds from corn hole tournament go to a charitable organization. The kids will love the Kid's Zone, with projects, games and crafts.

Shaky Beats Music Festival
May 5-7, 2017

Now you can live the line, "Share a Coke® and a Song" for a full weekend at the Shaky Beats Music Festival. Listen to favorite songs played by their DJ and refresh yourself with your favorite flavors of Coca Cola®.

Spend quality time with family and friends. Record a lip sync video and show off your dance moves.

9. Safety in Atlanta

Atlanta covers a great deal of area and is a large metropolitan city. Take normal precautions as you would in any big city. Don't leave valuables in your car, and watch your purse or wallet (don't leave them laying anywhere).

A few specific details:

Lots of people are comfortable riding the mass transit (MARTA) buses and trains at night. They are usually safe. If you're a female and alone, you might wish to choose a different mode of transport later in the evenings. Daytime travel is quite safe.

Driving on the interstate is safe, but if you're not used to driving in large cities, it can be worrisome. The interstates seem to be either stopped in gridlock (during rush hour) or flying by at twice the speed of sound. Drivers doing 80 is not an unusual sight. Stay in the right and middle lanes if you don't want drivers rushing up behind you.

There is not a lot of notice before exits on the interstates, so watch for your exit and watch for people trying to make last-second lane changes.

The downtown area is pretty deserted after dusk. Be cautious when walking or parking. There are panhandlers in the downtown area. Take a taxi if you head out, and stay on well-traveled sidewalks.

You may see individuals that look a bit like police, but with different uniforms - specifically, uniforms with helmets that resemble safari hats. These are people in the Ambassador Force of Downtown Atlanta. They help in patrolling the streets and can access police directly if you need them. They will happily escort you wherever you want to go. If you need directions, they are also happy to help in that area.

Buckhead has high end restaurants, businesses and shopping. So they do have some petty crime there. Exercise caution when you leave your car or return to it after shopping. Strolling from your hotel down Peachtree to shop or eat is very safe, day or night.

Outside the Atlanta perimeter (outside I-285, especially on the North side) the areas are considered quite safe. These areas are largely suburban. They include a shopping and business district that is safe to walk in. However, the sprawl of the area means it is usually easier to drive.

What Areas should you avoid?

Areas west of midtown and downtown and south of downtown are areas you may want to avoid. However, the Westside area by Howell Mill Road is a great area for shopping, and food and drink.

Health

There are not many health concerns specific to Atlanta. The water is safe and there are not any widespread communicable diseases.

If you have allergies or respiratory issues, take note that, although Atlanta has very little heavy industry, they do have many cars on the roads, so the air quality can be low. Posted and reported advisories for air quality recommend days when young children, the elderly and people with respiratory issues should limit or avoid activities outdoors.

Everyone in your party should stay as well-hydrated and cool as they can during the hottest months, usually from May to August.

10. Conclusion

Atlanta is a charming and beautiful city. It is rich in history and has many attractions that will always give you something to do. And when you're done, there are lots of great places where you can eat.

It was difficult to come up with the top things to see and do in Atlanta, because the city offers so much.

There are lots of travel guides that point out all the attractions in town, but this guide is pared down, so that you can see lots of interesting places, even if you only have a few days to spend here.

It should be relatively easy for you to find lodging and restaurants, since this guide breaks them down by budget.

We hope this Atlanta Travel Guide has inspired you to head out and find your niche in the busy, bustling, beautiful city of Atlanta.

Printed in Great Britain
by Amazon

45855324R00036